Snow-touched Imaginings

Snow-touched Imaginings

Poems

DAVID JAFFIN

First published in the United Kingdom in 2019 by
Shearsman Books
50 Westons Hill Drive
Emersons Green
Bristol BS16 7DF

Shearsman Books Ltd Registered Office
30–31 St. James Place, Mangotsfield, Bristol BS16 9JB
(this address not for correspondence)

www.shearsman.com

ISBN 978-1-84861-665-3

Distributed for Shearsman Books in the U. S. A.
by Small Press Distribution, 1341 Seventh Avenue, Berkeley, CA 94710
E-Mail orders@spdbooks.org
www.spdbooks.org

Production, composition, & cover design: Edition Wortschatz,
a service of Neufeld Verlag, Cuxhaven/Germany
E-Mail info@edition-wortschatz.de, www.edition-wortschatz.de

Title photograph:
"Eisblumen", by Hannelore Bäumler, München

Printed in Germany

Contents

9

With continuing thanks for
Marina Moisel
preparing
this manuscript

and to Hanni Bäumler
for her well-placed photograph

If I had to classify my poetry, it could best be done through the classical known "saying the most by using the least". The aim is thereby set: transparency, clarity, word-purity. Every word must carry its weight in the line and the ultimate aim is a unity of sound, sense, image and idea. Poetry, more than any other art, should seek for a unity of the senses, as the French Symbolists, the first poetic modernists, realized through the interchangeability of the senses: "I could hear the colors of her dress." One doesn't hear colors, but nevertheless there is a sensual truth in such an expression.

Essential is "saying the most by using the least". Compression is of the essence. And here are some of my most personal means of doing so turning verbs into nouns and the reverse, even within a double-context "Why do the leaves her so ungenerously behind". Breaking words into two or even three parts to enable both compression and the continuing flow of meaning. Those words must be placed back together again, thereby revealing their inner structure-atomising.

One of my critics rightly said: "Jaffin's poetry is everywhere from one seemingly unrelated poem to the next." Why? Firstly because of my education and interests trained at New York University as a cultural and intellectual historian. My doctoral dissertation on historiography emphasizes the necessary historical continuity. Today we often judge the past with the mind and mood of the present, totally contrary to their own historical context. I don't deny the past-romanticism and classical but integrate them within a singular modern context of word-usage and sensibility. Musically that would place me within the "classical-romantic tradition" of Haydn, Mozart, Mendelssohn, Brahms and Nielsen but at the very modern end of that tradition.

My life historically is certainly exceptional. My father was a prominent New York Jewish lawyer. The law never interested me, but history always did. A career as a cultural-intellectual historian was mine-for-the-asking, but I rejected historical relativism. That led me to a marriage with a devout German lady – so I took to a calling of Jesus-the-Jew in post-Auschwitz Germany. For ca. two decades I wrote and lectured all over Germany on Jesus the Jew. Thereby my knowledge and understanding of both interlocked religions became an essential part of my being. History, faith and religion two sides of me but also art, classical music and literature were of essential meaning – so many poems on poetry, classical music and painting.

Then Rosemarie and I have been very happily married for 58 years now. Impossible that a German and Jew could be so happily married so shortly after the war? I've written love poems for her, hundreds and hundreds over those 58 years, not only the love poems, as most are, of the first and often unfulfilling passion, but "love and marriage go together like a horse and carriage". Perhaps too prosaic for many poets?

When did I become a poet? My sister Lois wrote reasonably good poetry as an adolescent. I, only interested in sports until my Bar Mitzvah, a tournament tennis and table-tennis player, coached baseball and basketball teams, also soccer.

My sister asked whether I'd ever read Dostoyevsky. I'd only read John R. Tunis sports books and the sports section of the *New York Times* so I answered "in which sports was he active?" She said, rather condescendingly, "If you haven't read Dostoyevsky, you haven't lived." So I went to the library for the very first time and asked for a book by this Dostoyevsky. I received *Poor People*, his first book, that made him world famous. My mother shocked to see me reading and most especially a book about poor people said, "David, don't read that it will make you sad, unhappy – we, living in Scarsdale, weren't after all, poor people. From there it went quickly to my Tolstoy, Hardy and so on. In music it started with the hit parade, then *Lost in the Stars*, then the popular classics and with 15 or 16 my Haydn, Mozart, Schütz, Victoria ... And then at Ann Arbor and NYU to my artists, most especially Giovanni Bellini, Van der Weyden, Georges de la Tour, Corot and Gauguin ...

But it was Wallace Stevens' reading in the early 50s in the YMHA that set me off – he didn't read very well, but his 13 Ways of Looking at a Blackbird, Idea of Order at Key West, Two Letters (in *Poems Posthumous*), Peter Quince at the Clavier, The Snowman ... and the excellent obituary in *Time* magazine plus the letter he answered some of my poems with compliments but "you must be your own hardest critic". That pre-determined my extremely self-critical way with a poem. Please don't believe that prolific means sloppy, for I'm extremely meticulous with each and every poem.

My poems were published in the order written and I'm way ahead of any counting … The poem is a dialogical process as everything in life. The words come to me not from me, and if they strike or possibly join-a-union then I become desparate, read long-winded poets like Paz to set me off – he's very good at odd times. Those poems need my critical mood-mind as much as I need their very specially chosen words – not the "magic words" of the romantics, but the cleansed words of Jaffin – Racine used only 500 words. My words too are a specially limited society, often used, but in newly-felt contexts.

O something very special: I have a terrible poetic memory. If I had a good one as presumably most poets, I'd write say one poem about a butterfly, and every time I see/saw a butterfly it would be that one, that poem. But I forget my poems, so each butterfly, lizard, squirrel … is other-placed, other-mooded, other-worded, other-Jaffined. That's the main reason why I am most certainly the most prolific of all poets.

Shakespeare is the greatest of us: his sonnets live most from the fluency and density of his language. I advise all future poets to keep away from his influence and the poetic greatness of The Bible.

Yours truly
David Jaffin

P. S.: As a preacher the truth (Christ) should become straight-lined, timelessly so, but as a poet it's quite different. What interests me most are those contradictions which live deeply within all of us, not only in theory, but daily in the practice. And then the romantics have led me to those off-sided thoroughly poetic truths that mysteriously not knowing where that darkened path will lead us.

Poetry Book 82

Why write a (3)

  a) prelude to my

  82nd poetry
  (yes 82nd)

  book because
  each book is

  b) like "that road-

  not-taken" be

  fore though
  familiarly

  pathed through

  c) a darkened

  woods of an
  unmistake

  able other
  wiseness.

Why do the *(4)*

a) Anglo-American

s usually pre

fer The Messiah
whereas the

b) Germans perform

far-more-often

Bach's Christ
mas Oratorio

Is it because
of a long-time

c) tradition

a more inti

mate familiar
ity or a mirror

ing of one'

d) s indigenous

historical
musical and re

ligious sensi
bilitie

s.

Space most *(4)*

a) always opens-

out new dimen

sions to my
closely-timed

b) sensibility

Have they be

come seasonal
ly complement

ary as animal

c) s caved-in

for a winter'
s sleep and

then opened–
out to an al

d) most unlimited

sense of their

world's newly
created appear

ances.

The French *(3)*

a) have long real

ized an eye–

sensing cul
ture perhaps

b) *in part be*

cause of their

once courtly display
ing appearan

ces Even their

c) *music colored*

to eye–
sensing self–

displaying
pleasure

s.

Händel's (3)

a) *Messiah crowned*

with those

fugally depth–
immensing chor

b) uses and their

lyrically com

plementary
finely–felt

arias A relig

c) ious-worldly

masterpiece
of vividly ex

tending–con
trast

s.

Comeback *(4)*

a) not only sport'

s teams inhabit

ing players
downed by drug

b) s and alcohol

or those per

sonally off-
course Comeback

s aren't real

c) ly a return

to their former
insecured past

but more like
a restart to

d) a familiar

but newly per

spectived per
sonal domain.

Yes flower *(4)*

a) s do sing es

pecially

those perform
ing in a

b) choir of

selective

ly unpreten
tious voice

d–appearan
ces not to

c) be heard

through their

self–intuning
colors if

listening

d) loud enough

engage one
in their eye-

sensing musi
cal pleasur

ings.

Experience (2)

a)d craftsmen

sense the

where-fore
s and where-

nots of a pre-
chosen dialog

b) ue interchange

ably adept

I and Thou
especially

responsive-
calling

s.

Are these (4)

a) *sky-bound*

chimnied

smoke–puff
s but a

b) *secular i*

mitation

of that God–
ascending in

cense that

c) *catholic*

s the believ
er's prayer–

thought
s to the

d) heavenly

Father's

scent–aspir
ing presen

ce.

These solemn *(2)*

a) ly self-express

ive winter

birds lined–
up on tele

phone wire
s perhaps

b) touch-communi

cating a mess

age we're still
unable to

personal
ly decipher.

I've no (4)

a) authentic

means of dis

covering my
daily invisi

ble time-hidd
en age If it'

b) s the way I

feel re-aged
on a daily

and time-in
pending

course I'm
mostly sourc

c) ed between

childhood

and last-breath
appearance

s or perhaps
s better-yet

the way I

d) sense other

s envision
me with their

own subjective
ly persuing–

perspectives.

Nervous

laughter
not only re

lativizes
what's genuine

ly humour
ous but create

s as well an
artificial

uneasy atmos
phere.

For Tony (4)

a) Clouds in their

spacious kalei

doscopic change
ability whether

b) flat-landed

Van Goyen

esque or nat
ively establish

ing inherent

c) time-sequence

s as with Con
stable display

a creative re
solve heighten

d) ing our own

less–certain

ed awareness
es.

Does the

writing-out
of these o

therwise lin
ed-up poems

a reserved
empty-spaced

need for fu
ture poetic-

recalling
s.

Why do (2)

a) these shining

left-over

rain-drop
s from yester

day's substan

b) tially continu

ous releas
ings remind me

of spring bud
s most untime

ly-sensed.

I'm not real (4)

a) *ly interest*

ed in counting–

them-out Pessoa'
s and Cid Corman'

b) *s prolific poet*

isings Quality

and theme-var
ied expressive

ness is what

c) *counted for the*

three-of-us
in a world

quite willing
to relinquish

d) its far-out

poetic-
inheritan

ce.

If my voice

remains (as
many have pre

sumed) unique
and authentic

it still's con
tinuing its

hard–won freed
om from my o

therwise-
self.

Some of us (4)

a) even we Jews

ourselves may

sense we feel
anti–semitism

b) prevailing

at each and e

very scent of
unpleasant do

ings but un

c) fortunate

ly our history
has recorded e

ver-repeating
examples of

d) that underly

ing anti-semit

ic Satanic snake-
like changea

bility.

An early winter (4)

    a) pastel-afternoon

with only one

witnessing
black raven at

    b) the very top

of the high

est neighbor
ing tree I don'

t realize what

    c) he's imagin

ing though
it may slowly

be intruding
into my own

d) *sense of a*

once most satis

fying express
ive–conscious

ness.

It's good to (4)

a) *be married these*

58 years to a

caring beauti
ful and faith

b) *ful wife with*

such a similar

sensibility
I know deep–

down somewhere

c) she could have

done better
but I'm glad

to reserve
that kind of

d) judgment

for her own

feminine-re
ceptivity.

This thorough

ly cloud-blown
afternoon'

s momentar
ily encompass

ing my self-se
curing though

uncertain
ing time-as

piring expan
se.

Writing too- *(2)*

a) much-at-once

may lessen

my concen
trated word

and thought
intensitie

b) s no longer

penetrating

those most
necessary

poetically-
sourced-expos

ures.

Stefan Lochner' *(3)*

a) s self-accomodat

ing sweetness

unable even to
look-up to the

suffering-cruci
fied Jesus may

simply be term
ed as Internat

ional Gothic
but his mental

c) ity very much

at odds with

what may be
considered as

realistic
ally Germanic.

Like word (3)

a) s that don't

quite fit in

to that cross
word puzzle

b) blackened

out from even a

tenuous reach
Friends how

ever common

c) ly situated

most depth
ed familiar

ity uncomm
only distan

cing.

She modest *(3)*

a) by nature re

vealed most

of her for
med unknown

b) past when we

sat the three–

of-us with an
alternate o

ther person
ed her not so

c) *equally sourc*

ed but still

for me time-
compelling

past.

Here now

when each tree
reclaims its

most person
al self oft

perfectly
rounded to a

receptive
ly complete

identity-
cause.

Church music (2)

a) too intent on

securing its

most specific
word-direction

ing may lose
the full-depth

b) of its music

al-expressive

ness as poetry
which tends to

say more than
it's actually

revealing.

Advent *(2)*

a) should intend

a reawaken

ing of our
Jesus-orient

ed faith not
only of past

b) fervor but

also in the

intense wait
ing for what

continual
ly remains un

finished.

His was a (3)

a) most recogniz

able face some

what like a
bull dog'

b) s though con

siderably

friendlier
We saw him

often at con

c) certs pacing

his lonely
steps to a

rhythmic un
ity.

She became *(2)*

a) impulsive

ly there the

eyes first
then those

self-certain
ing hand

b) s ready to

preach her own

most existen
cially exper

ienced inspok
en truth

s.

Even Schumann' *(5)*

a) s fine Piano Quin

tet suffered

(especially the
two last move

b) ments) being per

formed after

Schubert's lyri
cally intense

F Minor Variat

c) ions No romant

ic music can
stand–up a

gainst his
death–invok

d) ing so repet

itively beauti

fying death–
nearing works

most always

e) complement

ary to his
inordinate

ly life-de
siring future.

Jochen Klepper (6)

a) a successful

national

ly-oriented
writer married

b) to a Jewess

poetized first-

rate Advent
music in 1938

the year of the

c) Night of Crystal

committed
suicide with

her 1942 with
out a possible

d) means of escap

ing from her

deportation
realizing

full-well as

e) a devout Christ

ian The Lord a
lone pre-deter

mines life and
death We all

f) live with such

unresolving

even daily-ten
sions?

Ernest Chausson *(5)*

a) as a typical French

composer alway

s on the creat
ive look-out

b) for addition

al eye-sensing

coloring
s his unusual

ly-sourced Con

c) certo for Violin

Piano and String

Quartet sound
ing at time

s like César

d) Franck and his

own previous

symphony but
with the con

cluding move

e) ment as bombasti

cally overdone
as Beethoven'

s choral 9th's
move

ment.

It's easy to (2)

a) take-out one'

s darkening

moods on the
nearby inno

cently unsus
pecting vic

b) tim But if it

becomes her daily

cost he may
react with a

venomous ser
pent's poison

ed–response.

Southern Flori (6)

a) da a most-like

ly winter re

sort for out–
worked and re

b) tired mideastern

ers yet it'

s as danger
ously mined

as post-war

c) Vietnam with

venomous ser
pents grassing

in your own
backyard not

d) to mention an

alligator or

two And that
Red Tide smell

ing and destroy

e) ing whole area

s of sea-shor
ed pleasuring

s and those not-
so-infrequent

f) hurricane'

s what and who

ever's chosen
for their so-

called idyllic-
Florida.

Without pre (4)

a) vious warning

music of more

or lesser qual
ity time-extend

b) ing hearing-

spells of eith

er my childhood
past or more re

cently concert

c) ed but they be

come heard in–
their–own–right

while yet de
scribing

d) my momentary

self–involv

ing raison d'
être.

Those dead (2)

> *a) friends of a*
>
> time-recall
>
> ing past seem
> to inhabit
>
> more of my
> present-day

> *b) conscious*
>
> ness than e
>
> ven my self–
> secluding
>
> dreams could
> realize why.

These process

> ional cloud
> s moving at
>
> their slow
> ly paced
>
> self–reassur
> ing time–se
>
> quences.

Why did that (6)

a) first-rate Eng

lish music end

with Purcell
or the Spanish

b) Golden Age

with Calderón

or the truly
great German

music with

c) Brahms And if

because of
their time

s why-weren'
t they suffi

d) ciently sourc

ed and if-be

cause of a
lack of call

ings why then

e) and there'

s also the
Romantics'

mostly earlied
inspiring

f) s as with a

ging men when

the life-bear
ing sap run

s dried.

First time *(4)*

a) I've been call

ed "a romant

ic" while as
piring that

b) bouquet of

small and viv

idly singable
flowers for

Rosemarie

c) as if all men

whether ro
mantically sourc

ed or not
shouldn't a

d) dorn their

loved-one'

s eye-indwell
ing kiss-worthy

needs.

These face *(3)*

a) less person

s from Macke'

s last paint
ings as he'

b) d become short

ly thereafter

in the trench
es of that

Great War
facelessly

c) killed and be

ing killed

by a face
less unseen e

nemy.

I may have

an-ax-to-grind
actually more

and many but
if used too

often they be
come blunted

through their
diminishing

cause.

These leaf

less tree
s seem to be

growing to a
shadowless

height of
my early morn

ing pre-tim
ed awaken

ings.

Rarely do

the la-la-la
fa-la-la a

rias of Bach
and Händel

match-up to
their contrast

ing contrapunc
tual choral out

pouring
s.

The first (3)

a) *chorus of Bach'*

s "O come you

heathen redeem
er" left me

b) *really spell-*

bound but the

succeeding
arias and re

citative
s express

c) ive more of a
Lutheran need
for saying-
it-most bibli
cally-correct.

Can this

only slight
ly-sensed

moon call
forth such

powerful ti
dal encompass

ings.

Who can (2)

a) possibly i
magine a God
who knows-it-
all sees-it-
all creates

b) and maintain

s the all
of our human

needs for a
self-emanci

pation.

Today's early

morning dramat
ically darkly

blue's land
scaping as of

an El Greco'
s religious

ly intensi
fying Toledo.

It may well *(4)*

a) be that women

more than men

remain as late-
comers by soc

b) cial engagement

s Be-that-

as-it-may at
times my poem

s without any
plausible ex

c) cuse leave me

waiting for

their most
necessary

word-exposure
s being better

d) and longer dress

ed in their

feminine way
for our on

coming poetic-
dialogue.

Woman's (5)

a) *ways remain*

for most men

hardly under
standable

b) *and that'*

s perhaps why

they entice
us with their

innocently

c) *underhand look*

s as caught
fish letting

the line loose
at times and

d) then holding-

it–tight as

with salmon
until we're

freshly caught

e) and netted to

their own spec
ial purposing

s.

I didn't ask (5)

a) for or real

ly need a 2nd

mother to help
guide my so

b) impractical

way through

the so-oft
disarming need

s of daily life

c) But there she

was as my
first mother

listening
(me) to her

d) every well-meant-

word but as with

mother-first
rarely follow

ing through

e) with their

well-minded
and certainly

most educative
where-with-

alls.

Trying to (4)

a) learn the necess

ary Greek for

the minister'
s role and now

b) Spanish at my

own desiring

s to read such
as Jiménez and

Borges in the
original but

c) I really fail

ed at both

as Sisyphus'
heavy load

that rarely
lightened

d) near the top

of finding

oneself back
down at the

very beginn
ing again.

Being honest *(2)*

a) with oneself

wasn't really

my special
problem but

that honesty
could become

b) at times a

way of not

changing what
had so burden

ed my own
outlook-on-life.

Some men *(3)*

a) have such a

dominating

way of pre
senting them

b) selves that

one need step

back at first
distancing

oneself be
fore reviving

c) once-again

I'm ready to

take this one
more-or-less

in–stride.

I imagine (3)

a) they're human

but they seem

more like phan
toms of the

future down–

b) look gadget

s and upstand
ing head-gear

hardly aware
who I am

passing them

c) flesh and blood

ed by with real
eyes nose and

threats all-of-
a-Shylock post

human humanity.

Looking *(2)*

a) through this

early morning

darkness as
a sea spread

ing out its tid
al invisible

b) voice within

the secluded

depths of our
now total a

wareness
es.

A new start (3)

a) even at this

time-altering

age as a
snake shedding

b) its outdated

skin A new

start invariab
ly satisfy

ing those pre-

c) timed but rare

ly conclus
ive time-shar

ings.

He was only (4)

a) 20 then but

he left on a

snow-impend
ing day all

b) that I had

to give of par

ental guidan
ce pre–formed

in my future
image of our

c) time-sharing

s he left
for the woman

of his future
life–sharing

c) s and for a

new family

quite other
wise than

our own.

Writing *(3)*

a) what's person

ally near yet

at a distanc
ing perspect

b) ive as if

what's exper

ienced could
become resour

ced even with

c) a lingering

feeling of
that alway

s what-could-
have-been.

No-so-often *(3)*

a) used-clothes

hung most dis

creetly in
the closet of

b) Pink's re-emerg

ing presence

ready for a
new start

having been

c) sanctified

from past not-
yet-dated pre

formance
s.

My old many- *(2)*

a) used-doctor

performing a

workable part-
time now a

ging from a
time-span that

b) retired us both

in need (as

he so aptly ex
pressed) for a

present time-
usefulness.

Her now age *(4)*

a) exactly the

same time-reach

of our made-
in-heaven marr

b) iage yet the

nearer she

came to in
specting my

facial skin

c) the greater

her so not in
nocently child-

like look
came approach

d) *ingly nearer*

to a forbidd
en kissed–

through tempt
ation.

Can the con *(3)*

a) *tinuous rain*

s wash these

dreamed–dark
nesses away

b) *as thorough*

ly cleansed

once the stol
en chalk's been

returned to

c) Miss Blackburn'

s 2nd grade black
board's time–a

vailing place.

Grey in *(4)*

a) grey this

indistinct

ive background
colorings e

b) ven of one'

s own self–decept

ive imagining
s Boredom the

continual in

c) activity of

an end–life
without a

meaningful
cause to un

d) easily sensed

remembranc

es and a slow-
down of a

self-motivat
ed purposing.

What's unsea (3)

a) sonable's now

becoming a

rule-of-thumb
as if the

b) rest of that

pre-determin

ing hand used
in the past

c) to an even-

flow of our e

ver-expecting
self-sufficien

ces.

Händel (with (3)

   a) the possible ex

   ception of Beet

   hoven)'s the
   most decisive

   b) of composer

   s What's said

   so emphatical
   ly so that

   one's left

c) little room

for backing–
away from its

self–avail
ing message.

He was sound *(2)*

a) lessly asleep

because that

sleep of his
had become

protective
ly so depth

b) ed that sound

s couldn't

penetrate
self-de

termining
enclosure

s.

Snow as in *(3)*

   a) the air be

   cause one could

   feel its pre
   determining

   b) cold-establish

   ing distan

   ces In the
   air yes but not

   yet soothing

   c) its ground-bas

   ed frost–
   wounded

   timely a
   waiting

   s.

Squirreling *(3)*

a) These small

black and suffi

ciently sourc
ed squirrel

b) s without the

slightest hesi

tation spring
from branch

to branch rare

c) ly if ever im

peded by 2nd
thought

s.

National (5)

a) istic militar

istic Germany

once the Europ
ean problem–

child has now

b) grown-up to

become its
most moralist

ic democratic
ally consist

ent spokes

c) man that its

so problem
atic past

has become al
most unrecog

d) nizable. I've

known many

young ladie
s quite early

grown-up to

e) their fully

womanly self-
image but

only one
young man

Cornell S.,

f) who at 16

seemed as
maturely ri

pened as a
time-suspend

ing apple.

A most strange *(8)*

> *a) ly endowed fam*
>
> ily The father
>
> about as unin
> teresting as

> *b) anyone I've e*
>
> ver met His
>
> wife a profess
> ional school-
>
> girl that one

> *c) imaged her*
>
> at best with a
>
> book-satchel
> on her grammat
>
> ically self-

d) sufficient

back 2 child

ren the daught
er a straight A

always learn

e)able scholar

until a ner

vous break–down
took her in

stride to that

f) downwards spiral

ling suicide

The son a
bad learner

morally and e

g) thically some

what out-of-
bounds but now

even-keeled
an apple drop-

h) down in his

self-sustain

ing father'
s mold.

A good thera (4)

a) pist requiring

most-of-all

empathy not a
pseudo-scientif

b) ic distan

cing but that

most necess
ary feeling–

for the pat

c) ient endanger

ing an object
ively sourced

lending–hand
that's not

d) squeezed-down

to its own

bone–prevail
ing self–stru

cture.

What makes *(2)*

> *a) a poem's hard-*
>
> to-say except
>
> its own pre-
> determin
>
> ing need for

> *b) a genuine*
>
> ly actuali
> zed impend
>
> ing self-suffi
> cient recept
>
> ivity.

Some person *(2)*

> *a) may leave*
>
> their mark-on-
>
> us often with
> out realiz
>
> ing why that
> interchange

b) able culture

al–intent

may also be
come comple

mentary as
well.

What we (2)

a) are wombed in

the darkness

of a mother
ly–dependent

time–hold yet

b) growthed to a

newly perspect
ived if self–

realizing i
dentity–

cause.

The window (2)

a) s of my life

prescribing

the distanc
ings of those

indwelling

b) depth-appear

ances as the
ocean's most

darkly inhabit
ing–claim

s.

Is our life'

s book more
like loose

pages that
must be bound

together to
tighten a

unity of its
as yet un

titled final
ity.

Finally *(2)*

a) freed from

that daily

learning a
Spanish vocab

ulary and
grammar that'

b) s failed to ap

propriate

the reconquis
ta of my own

linguistic
insufficien

ces.

Early life' *(3)*

a) s span as a

favored child

only son
youngest of

the three

b) affection

ate and loving
as spoiled as

one can imag
ine after the

form-recalling

c) Bar Mitzvah the

dark decade of
his finally recon

ciling that vast
ly unexpect

ed self.

Lights-on (3)

a) windowed a

cross-the-way

an equal div
ide family of

3 not alway

b) s visible cat

s and a fam
ily of equal

ly sizing–up
those night–es

caping cat'

c) s witness

ing eyes an

awareness all–
of–their–own

unfamiliar kind.

That same *(4)*

a) melody Schu

bert's F Minor

Fantasy contin
ued to phantom

b) us both into

a world of such

a depthed–per
petuating sad

ness that could

c) n't (despite a

lengthened
life–sustain

interlude) fin
ally reconcile

d) that tension

ed life and

death–dual
ity.

I can't rememb *(6)*

a) er the con

text or even

that unknown
personed "be

satisfied

b) with what you

have" She un
known to me

couldn't possi
by have known

the so–much I'

c) ve been bequest

ed nor my lin
gering dissatis

fying self-di
vided soulless

d) response Each

generation

seems to real
ize anew its

commanding

e) first-birth

ed rites (right
s) as if their

family and nat
ion had just

founded their

f) undeniable i

dentity–cause
timeless and

yet self-in
habiting.

That favor *(3)*

a) ed self-suffi

cient phras

ing and that
most personal

b) intimate re

sponse a Mozart

ean duality
pervading his

most especial

c) piano concerti

and even his
similarly-form

ed other con
certi as well.

Some poem

s change direct
ion while still

in the mid–
stream of dis

covering their
truly appro

priate yet oft
hidden themat

ic express
iveness.

Some short- (4)

   a) lived composer

   s and most es

   pecially Mozart
   seem almost

   b) time-fulfill

   ing whereas

   Schubert's unique
   ly lyrical gift

   seemed more like

   c) half-lived and

   Pergolesi's and
   Arriaga's nipped–

   in–the–bud of
   their so short

d) ly self-encom

passing winter

ed–flower
ings.

She possess (3)

a) ed a most a

dept profess

ional smile
that her a

b) gile lip

s seemed to

be coursed in
2 opposite

direction
s the one

c) pleasantly

personal the

other profess
ionally money–

oriented.

Two choice *(4)*

a) s but both haz

ard with a con

tinuing loss
The one pursu

b) ing almost an

imitation

of what no
longer satisfy

ing the present–
day political

c) course The o

ther dynamical

ly returning
to a one–sid

ed 16 years
past abandon

d) ing course

which to chose

in a loss–loss
situation.

The political *(4)*

a) concepts of con

servative and

liberal quite
clearly American

b) ly resolved in

the past Eng

lish Burkean
tradition

but in Germany

c) they've meta

morphed in
to what's be

come complete
ly different

perhaps because

d) the landscap

ing's histori
cally so other

wise sourc
ed.

This pre- *(3)*

a) Christmas

land's awaken

ing from a
dreamless

sleep with
only a relent

b) lessly half-

shaped moon

and the un
touchable dis

tancing of un

c) explored star-

realms to
guide its self–

emerging
course.

Christmas Carols *(6)*

"O little *(3)*

a) town of Bethle

hem" became

then the per
sonal creat

b) ive source of

the entire

world's unprece
dented longing

for its anoint

c) ed king

dom of eter
nal peace and

brotherly
love.

"Joy to the

World" even
nature and the

heavenly angel
s pre–attun

ed to His
sanctified

coming.

"How shall I (3)

a) receive Him"

a most person

al question
ing of our

b) heart's unful

filling desire

s for a re
deemer from

those self–en

c) compassing

forces of sin
guilt and death'

s eternal pre
sence.

"Hark the Her (2)

a) ald Angels sing"

well beyond
their heaven

ly source and
our lesser dark

ening earthly

b) realm of a re

demption for
all that was

that is and
shall be incom

ing.

"O come all (2)

a) *ye faithful"*

the credo

hymn for all
believing

persons and
their timeless

b) *ly self-resolv*

ing awaiting

for their per
sonal and yet

all–encompass
ing earthly-re

demption.

"God bless (2)

a) *ye merry gentle*

men" recalling

the Adam–in–us
and his self–

responsive
call to guilt

112

b) sin and death

while denying

The Good Lord'
s self-delimit

ing command
ments.

The world of (2)

a) our otherwise

self–determin

ing tempta
ion's gone

lost while

b) Christ become

s birthed to

our and its
newly conceiv

ed beginning
s.

Silent Night

's almost pre-
Raphaelite

sentimental
ity still mood

s the very re
vered still

ness of our
own blessed-re

ceptivity.

Because it' (2)

a) s natural does

n't imply

that it's
good as well

becoming sourc
ed to one'

b) s instinctual

behaviors

us at certain
crucial time

s helpless
ly self-depend

ent.

114

Trying to

explain faith'
s more like

revealing the
why of those

pre–establish
ing gift'

s indwelling
calling

s.

Each of us (3)

a) *while maintain*

ing our own

special way
s as long as

b) *they don't im*

pose on other

s and that
most personal

realizing if
they're mine

c) they can be

come yours–

as–well just
give them a
2nd–try.

The Magi *(3)*

a) Although

they well–re
alized they'

d been track
ing–out un

familiar

b) ground they

continued
neverthe

less as if
there had be

come no–other–

c) way than follow

ing that guid
ing-star to

the propheti
cally-recalling

Bethlehem.

Faith doesn' (3)

a) t mean as some

would–like–to–

believe giving
up one's own

b) specially

self–situat

ing freedom'
s way from

those other
wise unanswer

c) able response

s to life birth

love and the
death of a

self–inhabit
ing future.

It remain (4)

a) s ultimate

ly a quest

ion of per
spective

b) s especial

ly when we

realize now
that our own

antenae's only

c) meant for a

limited sen
sual response

to things
that appear

d) different

ly when scienti

fically obser
ved.

As a liberal (4)

a) Jew I sang

those Christ

mas carols at
the duly and

b) highly treed

communal–gather

ing at the lo
cal police

station on

c) Central Avenue

And I sang not
only voiced but

souled into
a pre–aware

d) ness of Christ'

s kingly but

as yet unnam
ed presence.

Rashomon *(4)*

a) that Japanese

movie of a

medieval hold–
up seen through

b) the varying

eyes of the

gangsters and
the otherwise

responses of

c) each of the

passenger
s that film

summed–up
the very essen

d) ce of histori

cally depthed–

understand
ings.

Only the wind

seems to realize
why it alone'

s prevailing
at such an in

tensely self–
satisfying

all–encompass
ing invisible

thereabout
s.

Wind what'

s the cause
of your invis

ibly-sourced
anger Have these

religious pre–
Christmas quiet

udes awakened
the wrath of

your heathen i
dentity-cause.

122

Awaken (3)

a) ing with this

early morning

stillness
Nothing move

s not even

b) the soundless

permanence
of these win

ter-bared bran
ches as if

time itself

c) had ceased

caring for
its daily

transform
ing aware

ness.

As I dream *(5)*

a) ed of Rosemarie'

s not yet self–

fulfilling
temptation

s (really of
my own) awaken

b) ing with a

feeling of be

ing betrayed
by my own un

easing other–

c) sided self

If dreams re
create what–

could–have–
been then

d) this one's

nothing more

than a red-
flag-warning

beware of your

e) endangered

beauty-satis
fying poetic

imaginat
ion.

Do children *(4)*

a) (the smaller

they are e

ven more-so)
love flying

b) kites as if

exploring

these vast
unknown space

s of their

c) self-indenti

fying person
and/or be

cause of those
insistent

coloring

d) s at the very

source of
their self–

attending
smiling-route

s.

False or fake *(7)*

a) news seems to

prevade not

only the media
It present

b) s only one

side to the

story leaving-
out the most

necessary

c) full-context

It's like our
good dean to

day preaching
a text Isaiah

d) 35 which like

so many pro

phetic text
s details Is

rael's future

e) whereas for our

good dean not a
word of that

Israel remain
s chosen but

f) without rhyme

or reason

False new
s has become

main–stream
democratic

g) churchify

ing in its

all–encompass
ing self-de

ception
s.

She that o (2)

a) therwise minist

er reminded me

more of a frog
little and jum

py intently
self-sourced

b) preaching as

if she'd found

that most wel
come leaf for

her so humane
accommodating–

message.

Advent with (5)

a) all the especial

ly lightful

trimming
s brightly arti

b) culating a seem

ingly wordless

message which
may have been

lost through

c) the ages remind

ing of my fath
er for the Columbia

football game
s everything

130

d) prepared most

important

the half-time
goodies but

alas he'd for

e) gotten those

most essential

ant entrance-
ticket

s.

Still life (2)

a) s require an

especially in

tense focus
dialoguing

a receptive

b) objectivity

spacing its
light–ascend

ing transpar
ently evolv

ing–message.

These lithe- *(3)*

a) barren high-

standing birch

trees softly
swaying to the

accords of

b) their wind-en

ticing femin
inely respond

ing appeal
s not unlike

Renoir's Dan

c) cers impulsing

a closely-sour
ced unifying

birthed-leng
th.

Lean day *(3)*

a) s the tree

s no longer

self-perpetua
ting a leafed

fullness of
out-spreading

b) in-spoken

protective

sheltering
s now bared

as aging men
of their life–

c) *trusting time-*

securing ex

tensive expect
ation

s.

Dynamical *(2)*

a) *ly coalesc*

ing stream

s of over-
lapping cloud

s as late Ro

b) *mantic French*

organ fuge
s substancial

ly up-lifting
their own spiri

tual potency.

These pene (3)

a) trating wind

s have final

ly lost their
a priori impetus

b) wherever se

cretly sourc

ed have now
settled-down

domesticat
ed to their

c) routine occas

ionly whisper

ing solitude
s.

A myster *(2)*

> *a) ious silence*
>
> as if even
>
> words them
> selves had be
>
> come untouch
> ably heard

> *b) scarcely defin*
>
> ing their only
>
> time-apparent
> continual
>
> ly evasive-
> cause.

He'd be *(2)*

> *a) come the so-*
>
> called prophet
>
> ic-type appear
> ing at irre
>
> gular rarely
> pre-determin

b) ing interval

s with a mess

age that had
become wordless

ly sourc
ed.

These process

ional cloud
s darkly inhab

iting what's re
mained an un

known myster
ious source

d to the wind'
s time–recall

ing appearan
ces.

Sleep's one- *(3)*

a) third reign of

our earthly re

conciling–
stay depthed

b) in a dream

ed–darkness

of time-evas
ively trespass

ing its un

c) certained

though contin
ually-redefin

ing origin
s.

Culture *(9)*

a) though encom

passing more

than its self–
inhabiting

origins could
possibly proof

b) the essence of

a people'

s historical
ly redefin

ing raison
d'être Each nation'

c) s marked by its

especial contri

bution to world-
culture The

d) Italians by

their canvass

ing a world
that still re

mains museum-

e) ripe The French

by their vis
ibly eye-sens

ing apparen
cies The Austr

f) ians and Ger

mans by their

musical self-
attunement

The proud

g) Spaniard

s by their
Don Quixot

esque self-i
rony The

h) English

and Russian

s by their
literary

i) psychologi

cally-depthed

human under
standing.

These rain (4)

a) s seems to have

become impulsive

ly aware of a
certain timely

b) acceptance

after such a

long dry-spell
One used to

say "there's a

c) time and a

place for most
everything"

but these rain
s seem to have

d) over-done their

once pre-deter

mining welcom
ing phase.

Why are the (8)

a) Germans and Eng

lish so rich

in quality
Christmas

b) carols espec

ially when com

pared with o
ther nation

s Were they

c) more religious

ly-depthed
than other

nations or es
pecially as

d) with the Ger

mans more music

ally-attuned
Strange to

say that Haydn

e) along with

Händel among
the very great

and least tragic
of composers

never wrote a

f) Messiah or Christ

mas Oratorio

to suit his
most Christmas-

sensed enlight
enment Why was

g) Brahm's overpower

ing Requiem

perhaps the last
of the truly

great religious
works Does that

h) vacancy mirror

the declining

depth of modern
spiritual

ity.

It snowed a *(3)*

a) gain in the

night as if

to remind us
of its still

b) Advent-like

purifying

qualitie
s while the

night respond

c) ed with a

somewhat
brighten

ing aware
ness.

It's "a dog' (3)

a) s life" here

better than for

most upstand
ing person

b) s in other

parts of the

world Animal-
love as with

those untouch
able ones in

c) the camp's dis

playing an e

ven lesser re
gard for those

death-rowed hu
mans.

I prefer a (2)

a) selected mem

ory (in my

case it seem
s there's no

alternative)
similar to a

b) life's view

weighted in de

grees of a
correspond

ingly tim
ed–relev

ance.

This early (2)

a) winter morning

however late

ly recalled
to a snow–

downed remem
brance that

b) seems more

like a corres

pondingly
pre–determin

ing light–
sufficiency.

As the Bible *(3)*

a) qualifies they'

re no reserv

ed seats in
Jesus' heaven

b) ly abode as in

my Malmsheim

er church
New-comers per

sonally awaken
ed even in

c) their latest

life-hours

to a most re
levant word-de

pendency.

This repetit (3)

a) ive snow's been

turned-on a

gain perhaps
s from an un

b) revealing

and yet purpos

ing hand or
has that dark

ly distanc
ing somehow

c) guilty appearing

cloud been call

ed to light
en its own

over-weight
ed burden.

If one be (2)

> *a) comes too pre*
>
> cise especial
>
> ly for its
> own sake it
>
> may well de

> *b) rive from*
>
> that precious
> sense of a
>
> too self-pur
> posing ap
>
> pearance.

He claimed (4)

> *a) to be "at a*
>
> loss for word
>
> s" perhaps be
> cause his so

b) self-emancipat

ing love could

n't be word
ed in that sort-

of-way and/

c) or because the

words themselv
es may have

kept a respect
ful distance

d) from such o

ver–ripened

expressive
ness.

Restraint (2)

a) *if genuinely*

sourced may

accommodate
itself to a

form-recept
ive intensi

b) *ty otherwise*

it could lead

to a sort of
academic-ac

ceptibil
ity.

This snow'

s faced with
an independ

ently-freed
child-like

playful
ness.

Sometime

s we're en
abled to feel

things much
the way o

ther's do es
pecially if

we've certain
ed a pre-sens

ed familiar
ity.

This snow (2)

a) man may have

had "a mind

of winter"
but however cer

tained he stood

b) to that cause

d a melting a
way into

the streams
of untold for

getfulness.

Sometime

s it's necess
ary to write

oneself in
to what may

seem at first
only tentative

ly-secured.

Today'

s snow (if it'
s so-named)

seems to be
intervalled

into less-
lasting phas

es of an in
determin

able respon
se.

A white Christ (4)

a) mas may seem

here momentar

ily necessary
because of its

b) mood-envision

ing perspect

ives whereas
Christmas in

the tropic

c) s needs little

or nothing of
that only the

Christ-child
sent by his

d) Father to re

deem our way

ward self-be
coming oft sin

ful way
s.

These leaf

less tree
s however lone

ly now embrac
ed by the

snow's culti
vating softness

es.

She came in *(3)*

a) to the eye doct

or's waiting

room with such
a proud upstand

b) ing-look that

I wondered if

that impend
ing operation

couldn't less

c) en her self-i

mage down to
its ground–

based assuran
ces.

This snow' (2)

s now reclaim

ing its home–

rights here–
to–stay as

long as it

b) does burying

those ground–
based nakedly-re

vealing o
pen–wound

s.

And now (3)

    a) with the new

    ly arrived

    snow reigned
    as far as

    b) the eyes

    could behold

    its self–as
    suming expan

    se as a new
    ly defin

    c) ing empire cer

    taining its

    once unfore
    seen border

    s.

Imperial China (5)

a) then muchly bey

ond the realm

s of European
imagining

b) s by the year

1000 hundred

s of years a
head of Europe

in most all

c) areas of a

cultivated
life with its

great 8th Cent
ury Tang dynasty

d) reaching such a

high level of

poetizing and
painting while

Charlemagne'

e) s Europe proud of

its growing
but still limit

ed ability to
read and write.

This newly *(2)*

a) felt snow

now inhabit

ing the leaf
less tree

s with a
finely-sens

b) ed alternate

appraisal

of such in
timately puri

fying landscap
ing-design

s.

I prefer *(4)*

a) that Christmas

song of a bor

der people
once German now

b) Polish offer

ing the newly

born Christ-
child a more

comfortable

c) winterly habit

ation and a
food-display

heavily digest
ible even for

d) its most hearty

welcoming in

habitant
s.

For Judith *(3)*

a) with many

thanks for such

an unusual Christ
mas card with

b) Joseph the Christ-

child in arms

and Maria behind
in bed reading

the Bible per

c) haps to make-

certain of
her child's pre

ordaining–
birth.

"Mind your (2)

a) (own) p's and

q's I take that

to mean for me
personally

mind your own
perspective

b) *s and quer*

ies and don'

t attempt to
impose them

on other
s.

In the midst (4)

a) *of nowheres-*

else–to–go

I took my
non-reserved

b) *place and wait*

ed (I couldn'

t at my ad
vanced age) re

member for

c) whom and/or

what but I
waited not-for-

long while time
itself seem

d) ed to have be

come my only

still avail
able compan

ion.

These long *(3)*

a) winter night

s seem sourc

ed with their
own time-length

b) ening impetus

that yields

only after a
distancing

light appear

c) s at its faint

ly self–inhab
iting horizon'

s calling
s.

A bleak win (7)

a) ter day's only

living sign

s these most
ly black–defin

b) ing birds sear

ching the hea

vens perhaps
s for a sign

of what could

c) possibly satis

fy their in
creasing hung

ried-need
s The snow

d) now kept

through the

frost-hold
ing ground-

base as if per

e) manently pre

senced as long
as this cold

would value
its timely–

f) sensed design

s This is a

time for
those Breughel

ian not only

g) children'

s games and
perhaps too

for those in
door warmly–

h) sourced re

flective-a

wareness
es.

It's not es *(7)*

a) pecially unus

ual now in

these economi
cally dependent

b) times that

children will

be brought up
by their grand

parents also

c) when many par

ents have been
killed in these

repetitive
blood-letting

d) wars that blood

s their child

ren to influen
ces as with

Martin Buber or

e) S. L. which may

possibly help
shape their de

signs for fu
ture calling

f) s escaping

the so oft ne

gative parental
examples of help

creating their

f) children in

the image of
their own

self-desir
ing expectat

ions.

Perhap *(6)*

a) s for those

who would
have chosen

their parent

b) s or child

ren otherwise
they may still

live-on through

c) their less-

familiar child
ren through

word-use
mannerism

d) s common

taste in this

or that and e
ven through

mood–contrast

e) s similar

time-sha
dowings and

much-else
which may pre

f) clude an all-

impending

otherwise
ness.

It's diffi *(3)*

a) cult to miss

friends how

ever-close
through certain

b) ed time-dis

tances as now

with Martin K.
dead after

last seen at

c) this time of

year a once-
a–year's-close-

friend now
one less

than that.

If Free-will (3)

a) down here earth-

bound doesn't

preclude an
all-knowing

b) God even of

our freely–

chosen way
s up-there

Two level
s of what

c) will and

should alway

s remain per
manently un

touchably o
therwise.

As we usual (2)

a) ly don't know

what's really

good for us
"Thy will be

done" while demo
cracy's will-of–

b) *the-people may*

lead (as de Tocque

ville propheci
ed) to a self-

deceptive tyran
ny-of-the-

majority.

This time-

clasping snow
blanks my mind

as Webern'
s from the

lesser detail
s of these

immovable
silence

s.

This snow'

s breathing
light into

my eye-search
ing distant

ly-awakening
time-recalling

s.

Why have

these time-se
curing house

s with their
so evidently

windowed ex
posures re

mained so
satisfy

ingly self-in
habiting.

These broken (3)

a) patches of snow

seem to be con

tinually ex
tending the

b) full-range of

my timely sen

sed-imagin
ings And it'

c) s also awaken

ing my "mind'

s eye" to its
windowed bright

ening–presen
ce.

Listening (*4)*

a) to old and

dear friend'

s daily and
most intimate

b) problems a

wakens either

an empathiz
ing how can

I possibly
help and/or

c) an encompass

ing boredom

(though silent
ly withhold

ing) Why can'

d) t we discuss

themes of act
ual relevance

for all-of-
us.

Listening *(4)*

a) to French classi

cal music es

pecially of
the impress

b) ionistic kind

may become a

convenient
escape-route

for German
s and other

c) s from the

most serious

intention
s of much

heavy-minded
German compos

d) ers to become

intimate

ly sourced to
such colorful

subtletie
s.

If my own I *(3)*

a) dentity'

s of an his

torically-
sourced Jew'

b) s home-find

ing express

ive INRI
It's also an

chored to the
tidally change

c) able rhythm

s of our most

self-certain
ing 58 year

young-marriage.

These all- *(4)*

a) kinds-of-tree

s have receiv

ed an inward
ly sensed-de

b) ciphering

of their time–

inclusive
years where

as we've been

c) given no such

apparent mean
s of realiz

ing the continu
ally otherwise

d) ness of our
fluently self–
encompassing
identity–cause.

If one (3)

    a) allows this
    lasting appar
    ently close
    ly–purposed

    b) snow to situ
    ate oneself a
    new It may
    prove (even
    through a se

c) condary self-

certaining)
refreshing

ly account
able.

It's become (4)

a) most difficult

to rediscover

the voice
s these now

b) bared tree

s have left

behind Once
I thought

they'd been

c) singing through

my long for
gotten dream

s but when I
awoke only

their bared

d) outlines re

mained visual
ly if thin

ly untouch
ably heard.

It may have

been the first
time this cool

ly distant Pro
kofiev awaken

ed in me a
depthed lyri

cal response
with his fade

away First
Violin Concerto.

I don't real (5)

a) ly know if

these darkly

out–spread
ing raven's

b) wings have

left behind

their shadow
ing resemblan

ce on snow

c) Breughel at

tuned them
almost mysti

cally resolv
ing with the

d) return of the

hunters But

even their
non–shadow

ings shadow
me with a

e) snow-remind

ing express

ive–conscious
ness.

This still

prevailing
snow's land

scaping anew
the depthed–

range of my
time–apparent

creative–imag
ining

s.

A continu (3)

a) ous display of

miraculous

happenings most
self-substan

b) ciating for a

faith badly in

need of such
shouldn't al

ways be seen
as a godly dis

c) play His con

stant imitator

saved Hitler
twice from his

pre-determin
ing death.

These street *(2)*

a) lights turned

on a once dark

ly inhabiting
war-like people

Now setting an
example for a

b) domesticat

ed self-satis

fying moral
izing other

wise-better
ness.

The post-Ro *(4)*

a) man Empire's

Europe as if

starting-up
all-over a

b) gain shouldn'

t be compared

(as many do)
to that high

ly enlighten
ed China of

c) the Song period

about 1000 rather

than empire for
empire's imper

ial decline

d) from their once

thoroughly
accomplish

ed radiat
ing fullness.

A dear very *(3)*

a) happily married

aging friend

once explain
ed (much to

my own aston
ishment) "I

b) love beauti

ful women" –

who doesn't
that women

have remained
for him much–

c) the-way ani

mals sniff–out

a prospective
time–sharing

mate.

My father *(4)*

a) (bless his mem

ory) rarely
called lawyer–

b) like a-spade-

a–spade most

especially
while inter

viewing pro
spective life–

c) mates for his

two feminine

children Other
wise he remain

ed a dreamer
daily attuned

d) to the wishful

thinking

of calling a
spade for ex

ample the queen-
of-hearts.

Balzac with (5)

a) his almost Eng

lish sense of

the social
realities of

b) his own time

s and people

once claimed
that great fort

unes were most

b) often the re

sult of a de
vious criminal

intent I would
counter with

d) the American

tycoon's almost

artistic imag
inings of fort

unes and im

e) provement

s no longer
pre-establish

ing.

Some may have (5)

    a) sensed (despite

    their more real

    istic experience
    s) that this

    b) snow's meant-

    to–stay as

    the Chinese of
    the Song period

    experiencing

    c) the Mongols'

    ravishing blood
    and territori

    ial taste for
    an unlimiting

d) expanse And yet

that great em

pire all-too-
soon melted

away as the

e) snow of its

irretriev
able time-tell

ings.

The fear (2)

a) she'll remain

as her mother

immovably in
bed with life

failing of
her slowly a

b) wakened

purposing a

no-wheres-
left of my

time-establish
ing person.

Those poem

s almost mid-
aired whose

most-chosen
words hadn't

as yet taken
to a fully

resounding
permanent

ly exposing-
resolve.

That word- *(2)*

a) flashy type as

Danny B. of

the equally
flaming red

hair seems to
be burning a

b) live with his

most necess

ary concern
s for self-im

portan
ce.

Even in (3)

a) time the snow

will become

so accomodat
ing to our

b) windowed land

scapings

that it will
remain only as

an indwelling
statically

c) necessary
back-ground'
s pre–estab
lishing phas
ings.

On such day (3)

a) s the cold re
mains as these
even less re
ceptive wind
s invisibly

b) certaining
the softness
of our flesh–
warmthed in
habiting sensi
bilities as

c) an intended

dialogue with
an indistin

guishable re
ceptivity.

Half-full (3)

a) or half-empty

are most cer

tainly not
the same It'

b) s a question

of perspect

ive 40 degree
weather feel

s totally diff
erently after

c) a heat spell

or when it'

s thawing
an almost

permanent
ly felt

freeze-down.

A poet (2)

a) may visual

ize these

scatter
ed patches-of-

snow as word
s or even

b) phrases that

need to be uni

fied into
a coherent

ly-alive poet
ic-expressive

ness.

Should these

elaborately
lights-up Ad

vent days e
ven when in

not-so-qualitiy
taste be seen

as a recept
ive response

to Jesus' light-
of-the-world.

I've come to

realize in
these cold pre-

establish
ing days the

preserving in
tensity of

such deadly
expressive

leafless still
nesses.

Berries *(3)*

a) usually remind

me of a close

ly-held Octob
er cool-down-

b) spell But these

in mid-Decemb

er as abstract
ly reassuring

a speechless

c) but still e

vident cause
their refined

coloring
s.

This cold

may remain in
visible yet

it's clothed
in the mute

appearance
s of snow

frost and
these time-sus

pending ici
cles.

I never could *(4)*

a) have become a

church poet

though a few
of them through

b) the ages have

partly trans

cended that
most limiting

calling The

c) church never

holy for me
too easily com

promising with
the changeable

d) and mostly un

holy so-called

spirit-of-the-
time

s.

Few leave *(3)*

a) s left hanging

their dried–

down timely
holding-on

b) s as so many

of these over-

aged men thin
ly and sap

lessly express

c) ive of a va

cantly self-
apparent

thought-
range.

Dark dream *(2)*

a) s have cloud

ed my daily

comforts with
such unimagin

able fear
s that I a

b) *woke as if*

to another

time and place
unsubstan

tially other
wise.

My poetic i *(2)*

a) *magining*

s once open

ing-out field
s of grained-

awakening

b) *s But now*

bared-down
to these spac

eously unre
solved-distan

cing
s.

Was Pergolesi' (4)

a) s unfinished

Marian Vesper

s of such an
uneven qual

b) ity because

it was complet

ed with work
s of his out

side their ori

c) ginal context

and/or because
that great compos

er himself died
at 26 still so

d) varied in the

quality of his

composition
al know-how.

These wind *(2)*

a) ing up and down

wooden stair

s of Rosemarie'
s life-span

paralleled with
my birth that

b) same year and

The Night of

Crystals my
death-warrant

but a year
later.

How far have *(2)*

a) these snowed-

down reaches

of silence
been accompan

ing us even

b) beyond the lim

ited-range of
our daily time-

encompass
ing precept

ions.

Is a good *(4)*

a) and solidly

based bibli

cal theology
a pre-requisite

b) for a genuine

ly heavenly-o

riented faith
or have our

good works an
equally justi

c) fying claim

or is such a

good faith
only realized

d) through the

Good Lord's

exemplary
and reclaim

ing judgment.

Has this so *(2)*

a) innocently appear

ing almost child-

like forsaken
ing snow begun

immensing my
solitary ground-

b) based imaginat

ion even to

the depth of
its darkly-

sourced womb
ed-inhabit

ings.

Sometime *(4)*

a) s a vaguely un

touchable

feeling over
comes me (es

b) pecially when

these star

s have dimm
ed my timely

sensed–awaken

c) ings) that this

now–self–cer
taining snow

has left me
behind search

d) ing-out a

more heaven

ly surround
ing identity–

cause.

For Rosemarie I *(3)*

a) Our love (how

ever time-en

compassing)
needs for me

b) a reassuring

only me only
you only us

as if time
could ever ex

c) tend bey

ond that self-

immersing most-
now compelling-

unity.

For Rosemarie II *(2)*

   a) Saying it

   just right
   (the where

   these word
   s feel as if

   homely-bless

   b) ed) can never

   become an alter

   nate identity-
   cause for our

   pre-determin
   ing oneness.

The way *(2)*

   a) some Spanish

   poets feel a

   bout their lyri
   cally encompass

   ing guitar can
   never become

b) (for me at

least) second

ary to the
poem's own

less apparent-
ascendan

cy.

Are really (4)

a) first-rate in

terpretive

artists perform
ing for their

b) audience and/

or for their

own lingering
sense-of-accom

plishment

c) or even poss

ibly for an
invisible God–

creator of
their own es

d) pecially pre-

establish

ing gift
s.

Listening *(3)*

a) to I've-heard-

it-all-before
Glazunov

Violin Concerto
(though those

b) moments of sus

ceptible beauty)

One looks for
another kind

of more modern
violin concerto

c) as those of

the otherwise

Prokofiev and
Weinberg's first

class Concerti.

Awakening a (3)

a) full week be

fore Christmas

to this early
morning snow

b) holding in

tact its immov

able presen
ce as if it

had become

c) the pre-estab

lishing sense
of timeless

distancing
s.

Haiku's *(for (4)*

a) Rudiger J.) re

mains depend

ent on an i
mage-sense

b) unified phras

ing But be

cause of its
strict form

those most

c) necessary

pivotal word
s remain lost

and forgott
en from their

d) own exacting

expressive-

need
s.

One should (4)

a) only write

sonnets when

its most de
manding form'

s pre-estab

b) lishing one'

s own mind-
set Otherwise

most unfortun
ately they'

ll leave the im
pression of an

c) excessive off-

balancing

indulging
for quite

the adequate

d) rhymes and

their yet hidden
adventur

ous meaning
s.

When an im (4)

a) passioned

love daily enrich

es the depth
of its self-

b) securing rai

son d'être

it will either
overcome in

Christ's

c) sense that al

ways impend
ing fear-of-

death or in
crease that

d) more intens

ing fear of a

permanent
loss.

Reading-bet *(3)*

a) ween-the-line

s may also

become a read
ing into

b) one's own sub

jectively

sensed–feel
ings or it

may help the

c) author's con

tinuous need
for a most–

personal dia
logue.

This snow (2)

a) s may also

voiceless

ly be speaking
to me of the

transient
nature of life'

b) s seasonal

ly ever-return

ing timely ex
pectant birth'

s so slowly
melting-away.

At the end (3)

a) (if one could

ever call it

that) after
having seen

and experienc

b) ed all that

met his eye'
s minding-ex

pectation
s he died in

to a calmed

c) breathless

ness irretriev
ably lost in

those vastly
unknown region

s.

If getting- *(3)*

a) things-done

has perhap

s only self-
perpetuat

b) ing cause

in the course

of such a tur
bulent know–

how he'd un
done as with

c) Humpty-Dumpty

even more of

what couldn'
t be put

back togeth
er–again.

Perhaps his (3)

    a) almost obsess

    ion for new
    discoverie

    s mostly in
    music mirror

    b) his own hope

    of being re

    discovered
    for a continu

    ing life-
    source even

c) *from his grave-*

down carefully

inscriptur
ed tomb–

stone.

Yes he de *(3)*

a) *sired a full*

ness of life'
s ever persist

ent calling

b) *s and (as*

well) a heaven
ly no reserv

ed (neverthe
less equally ex

c) pectant) two-

seat timeless

ly left–over
s.

With those e (3)

a) mancipated

Moslems I feel

myself divid
ed right–down-

b) the-middle

(as America

has always be
come) for their

blood-letting
of a danger

c) ous (for Christ

ians and Jews)

idol now pre
suming with a

new godless
poise.

It's those (3)

a) *most always*

fully-toothed

models smil
ing-me-down

b) *to my still*

activating

cavities and
those hold

ing-fast

c) to my dentist'

s supremely
self-oriented

satisfact
ions.

Early morn *(3)*

a) ing when the

poem itself'

s not fully
awakened

while I only

b) half-present

waiting impat
iently for

those particul
arly chosen

most-necess

c) ary word-image

s to set-off
my not alway

s so self-ap
parent mind–

set.

A lone o *(3)*

a) ver-sized ra

ven situated

at the very
top of the

highest vacant

b) ly-felt leaf

less tree wit
nessing the

morning's pre-
determining

ascent to the

c) still unknown

regions of my
mind's stead

fastly awaken
ing soul-

sense.

This cold'

s most demand
ing time-hold

's impending
no-where'

s-else but
this voice

lessly self-
distinguish

ing now.

Wood-knot (2)

a) s remain blood

lessly self-

apparent de
fining their

always pre

b) sent branches'

cut–off–
from–life'

s painful–
uncertaint

ies.

A woman' (3)

a) s beauty as

much an un

authorized
gift as the

b) poet's under

lying word–

sense left
my always as

tutely–thought
ful Uncle Irving

c) in Rosemarie'

s presence

stuttering–
for–express

ion.

Some familie (3)

a) s as the

modestly–shy
Uncle Irving'

s love–match
with the opera–

b) loving sensu

ously attuned

Aunt Nicki
would have work

ed–well except
for their hard

c) ly brought-up

children event

ually brought-
down to that

most inevitable
lower-level.

What make

s some people
tick may only

become fully
understand

able through
the minute

hand's pre-de
termining

know-how.

These light-

blue curtain
s may close-

off the sun
with only

the touch of
an indwelling

hand's length
ening-depth

of a shadow
ing-response.

Watching (2)

a) this sun-shin

ed ice-crust

ed snow melt
ing away its

pre-determin

b) ing time-lim

iting once-of-
having-been

so particul
arly jewel-de

signed.

"The rest is (2)

a) silence" though

that Shakespear

ean silence
remains voiced–

as–well having

b) witnessed

the bloody–
end of what

once seemed
so readily–

intact.

So-called (2)

a) successful

men's most com

petitive na
ture must re

main toned–
down to a

b) commonly invok

ing language

if friendship'
s to become of

an inherent
ly lasting

value.

If (as Buber (4)

a) rightly claim

s) an all-en

compassing
dialogue's

b) daily surround

ing our more-

or-less fruit
ful express

iveness then an

c) old and lone

ly man with
no–one–else

to inspire his
endemic self-

pity's dialog

d) uing that as

well with his
daily self-re

flection
s.

Writing with (3)

a) a daily work-

load in mind

as with my
not–so–favor

b) ed Thomas Mann

may be perhap

s half-correct
ly identified

as bourgeois
Rather it ex

c) pends a pre-

inherent value

for a fully
self-identify

ing crafts
manship.

Snow on the *(2)*

a) ground snow in

the air snow–

streams of
light denying

whatever dark
nesses had ac

b) cumulated in

her aging but

still resilent
ly-kept time

ful-remembran
ces.

Nice in our *(3)*

a) favorite Ital

ian restaur

ant Rosemarie
all blond and

b) sweetly smil

ing my way and

I hers as we'
d remained

after 58 year

c) s together

in that same
youthfully

reminding
love-length.

Can one ex (10)

a) pect a Polish-

Jewish composer

b) as Weinberg

twice saved

from the Nazi
s and once

from Stalin with

c) his immediate

family murdered
to write only

beautifully
lyrical music

d) Can one ex

pect a now
"Russian"

composer liv
ing in a land

e) attacked by a

murderous

band of savage
s to just sit–

back and music

f) ally contem

plate the beaut
ies of a God–

created world
Weinberg wrote

g) what he had

to with no

aesthetic ex
cuse for its

at times bombast

h) ic self-defen

sive emotion

al outpour
ings but he

also wrote of

i) the other side

of life rare
ly his for that

most necessary
soulful enjoy

j) ment of it and

our needs for

his depthed–
felt beautify

ing antitode
s.

Art of most (8)

a) any kind can

also become

a self-defen
sive means of

b) protecting

oneself again

st the dark
er-side-of–

life not only

c) dwelling out

side but well-
within our

own self-in
habiting depth

d) ed-darkness

es It's more

effective
than walls (es

pecially that

e) Chinese one)

that rarely
helped se

cure its own
peaceful and

f) cultural pre

sense As art

ists (the real
ly good one

s) most usual

g) ly realize

their gift

was also giv
en as a most

personal re

h) sponse to

suffering
and death's

always await
ing pre-deter

mining time.

Macbeth *(5)*

a) not in the

original in

comparable
Shakespear

b) ean language

and with only

60% hearing
still ranged

to that un

c) fathomable

depth of evil
's reign over

an almost un
limited person

al and imperson

d) al destruct

ive intensity
and a society

however lamed
still equipped

to reestablish

e) its once again

peacefully
necessary some

how God-given
daily-exist

ence.

These last (4)

    a) remnants of

    snow however

    tenacious
    ly cold–kept

    b) for self-re

    liant purpos

    ings now slow
    ly melting a

    way But not

    c) so with that

    9th grade Emer
    son essay that

    has remained
    with me all–

d) these years

to that act

ualizing
ever–present

now.

Most every (5)

a) where I go

"All the pow

er to you"
may feel a

b) bit differ

ently as a

sensitive
aging and some

what frail

c) poet Yes the

language'
s poetry is

unquestion
ably strong

d) now and then

but that's

not really me
but the other

side of a self-

e) dialoguing

dreamed–rever
ied or–what–could–

have–possibly–
been.

They looked (9)

a) *at me as if*

I were a crimin

al First the
receptionist

b) *started putt*

ing words in

my mouth that
didn't fit

just right

c) *Then the two*

assistant
s appeared in

the way one
prepares for a

d) funeral Finally

the boss himself a

cracker-jack
dentist espec

ially at the

e) monied-end

"Where is it"
He looked as

if I should
be prepared

f) for a finan

cial funeral

but about 10
long long min

utes after re–

g) searching the

waste–paper–
basket my dear

wife here–of–
the–day found

h) it just right

to be re–toot

hed again Rare
ly had my so

impractical

i) self-image

been so en
tirely tooth–

deposited.

Some chair *(6)*

a) s seem espec

ially appropri

ate for my
sit-down age

b) in my case

for example

the ones with
a most support

ive back-hold

c) But others

as the one
at the dentist

however read
ily readjusted

d) for my comfort

seem most de
cidedly pre-

pained Chair
s of my sit–

e) down age de

termine even

more than
they self-real

ize the length

d) and depth of

self–comfort
ing perspect

ives.

Some women (2)

a) (age matter

s little here)

become so ob
sessed for ap

pearance-sake
that one wonder

b) s if that ap

pearance hadn'

t become a
2nd-self meas

uring the dis
tance to that

finely-sensed
real-one.

Those most in (3)

a) terested in

the private

life of other
s who read

b) that so-call

ed boulevard

press have u
sually put–

off any at

c) tempt to own-

up to their
own failed

really pri
vate life.

Some day *(3)*

a) s as this

one pass in

their own
necessary

b) time-length

and leave me

lesser word–
light for

addressing

c) their most in

timately–held
private self–

expectant de
sign

s.

That short- (3)

a) length fall

neverthe

less left me
bruised to the

b) lower-level of

my upstanding

self-support
There pained

at the long–

c) dead big toe'

s newly-sour
ced receptive

life–claim
s.

Even though *(2)*

a) I'm quite often

up–in–arms a

gainst some of
my more ob

vious practi
cal weakness

b) es stay-put

right–where–

they–are quest
ioning my less

than self–e
vident sincer

ity.

Those of us (2)

a) long-retired

would prefer

their soft–
seated perhap

s well-earned
comforts may

b) realize in

times have

changed–down
to those hard–

minded irreduc
ibly no-turn

ings-back.

Narrative *(4)*

a) poems not-u

sually my–

kind–of–thing
become quite

b) often hardly

distinguish

able from
the poetic–

prose of an

c) Adalbert Stift

er or Joseph
Roth I'd per

haps prefer
writing on

their time

d) both sides of

those ever-so-

personal go-
ahead sign

s.

After hearing the Messiah (4)

a) There's so

much loving

intimate-ten
derness in

b) some of Händel'

s arias and

such a majest
ic strength in

his great con

c) trapuntal

choruses that
he's certain

ly an equal
of his some

what other

d) wise rival

Bach's usual
ly lonely ped

estalled-pri
macy.

A penny-a- *(2)*

a) line that's

the real worth

of much of to
day's poetry

neither philosoph
ically-depth

b) ed nor mood-

sensed void of

the very least
of word–imag

ining
s.

An aging marr *(3)*

a) iage 58 year

s to date

keeping each
other healthful

ly intact'

b) s unlimited

feelings for
those not–so–

limited extra
hungs and kiss

es while e

c) ven realizing

the other's
needs in one'

s own self-
mirroring

s.

December *(4)*

a) 21ˢᵗ's dark

nesses lower

ed-down to
their time-

b) prevailing

reach while

the December
sun's only

horizoned
to its own

c) most-limit

ing extent

Christmas
in the air

and in one'

d) s own mind-

set full of
its wonderous

ly light–evok
ing presence.

Shakespeare' (3)

a) s sonnets hard

ly original

in their time–
deriving rais

on d'être It'

b) s the fluency

and depthed–pur
posings of

their unique
ly poised–lang

uage that en

c) ables the best

of them to
stand alone to

such unapproach
able height

s.

Why in the (4)

a) Christmas

season of

light and hea
venly peace

b) ful-evoking

times so many

suicides so
intensed the

lonely forsak
enness of the

c) aging There

must be o

ther force
s at hand

here denying

d) The Good Lord'

s own eternal
and yet time-

prevailing
offering

s.

It may seem (3)

a) *strangely true*

that even athe

ists and agnos
tics often

b) *feel themselv*

es transform

ed in the
Christmas sea

son's light
ful presence

c) *and peaceable*

resolution

of man's so
self-destruct

ive undoing
s.

Even I an *(4)*

a) individual

ist by trade

though a Christ
ian in-heart

b) somehow feel

an especial

belonging
ness in this

season of

c) Christ's illu

minating birth
while the Channu

kah candles
being lit for a

pre–determin

d) ing victory

for the fu
ture Christ'

s oncoming-
triumph.

He wrote him (2)

a) self dry as

those mount

ain stream
s in the sum

mer of their
unspoken i

b) magining

s Nothing left

to be said
rock-depth

ed silent
ly-indwell

ing.

Open field (2)

a) s distanc

ing one's

thought
s beyond those

limited hori

b) zons of daily

use to the
wood's darkly

encompassing
no-wheres-else-

but-then.

He with the (3)

a) darkly rimmed

intellectual

glasses She
more like a re

ceptive I'm for

b) you and no

where's-else
A world of two

undivided at
its eye's cent

ering scope.

It rained a *(2)*

a) gain perhaps

because it had

nowhere-else-
to-go day and

night after
such a long

b) dry-spell per

haps evening-
out a now

thoroughly
completed-

wholeness.

Call it a (4)

a) *house if you*

like it per

haps because
it looked that

b) *way or what*

should have

been one until
his sickness

lowered–him–

c) *down but now*

it had be
come a provi

sorium with
one old used

d) chair and noth

ing else to

greet impend
ing visitor

s.

Ode to the *(6)*

a) Great Bard

It's not easy
to realize

when one play

b) with its spec

ially chosen
actors and act

resses has
competed its

c) staged-calling

and another

one has tak
en its pre

vious place

d) My mother al

most 105 cer
tainly out–

lived all
those pre-es

e) tablished cur

tain-calls but

then it's seld
om a complete

denial of the
previous play

f) but somehow a

continuity

at the very
least of the

stage–itself.

Now on Decem (3)

a) ber 22nd at 7:30

a complete

darkness Time
may have taken

b) its own pre-

determining

route though
this darkness

identifying
nothing else

c) than a depthed-

reaching into

those undiscov
ered realms of

one's very-be
ing.

Has this un *(3)*

a) timely but still

strongly self-

declaring wind
challenging

b) time's persis

tently samed-

sequences as
my father ada

mently rushing
well-ahead-of-

c) time for the

first possible

train to his
then newly

decorated off
ices.

Still some (3)

a) thing mysterious

about these car

lights artifi
cially pursu

b) ing through a

wooded road

perhaps into
the density of

a post–dated

c) Shakespear

ean linguist
icly accumulat

ing deadly–call
ings.

Does each in *(4)*

a) dividual death

of our close

friends Michael
B. Hans E. and

b) Martin for example

annul those

fruitful year
s of a common

ly sourced compan

c) ionship or have

they been stor

ed (as Viktor
Frankl thought)

somewhere in

d) the slowly for

gotten archive

s of timeless
reference-

work
s.

It may have *(4)*

a) remained the

same window

ed-view here
in Illmensee

b) of time's

changeable

routes but it
persists for

a rewording

c) of the poet'

s agile pen
and its own

not complete
ly still de

d) ciphering

seasonal sen

sibilitie
s.

With the *(6)*

a) usual at

his favored

gourmet rest
aurant look

b) ing for those

seldom theme

s we share in
a less than

commonly-held

c) sensibility

Shakespeare'
s Macbeth

newly staged in
Munich at least

d) provided a full-

hour of equal

ly prevailing
acceptibil

ity But then

e) (perhaps inspir

ed by those 3
witches) the con

versation attun
ed to his u

f) sual diabolic

ally inspired

otherwise
ness.

This rain' *(2)*

a) s fully flour

ishing wind-

blown present
s a scene

almost as

b) chaotically

sourced as
Lady Macbeth'

s blood–with
holding hand–

reach.

With his *(4)*

a) two biblically-

sourced minister

ial friend
s and his

b) Goethe-like pre

or post–Christ

ian "enrighten
ed faith" seem

s more like

c) a gracefully

frightened
deer on the

run with those
fire scent

d) ing his always

s devious

get–away endur
ance path

s.

Channnukah (10)

a) a festival of

light and peace

A victory o
ver the ene

b) mies' other

wise superior

reaching e
ven into our

daily life

c) imitating

their names
their dress

their most-e
verything–

d) else as now

Christmas

a festival of
light and peace

first for the
chosen-one

e) 's denying

Christ's in

visibly other
wise kingdom

INRI.

So many *(5)*

a) (for them) un

decipherable

symbols as the
Christmas tree

b) of life and

truth-stars but
rarely the Star

of David that
led the way

c) for those Baby

lonian astrolog

ers Exchange of
gifts in the

best of Channu
kah's tradition

d) Christmas

cards rarely

displaying Mary
and Joseph with

the Christ-child
in the cradle

e) Ox and ass

seemed to have

understood
better than so–

called Christ
ian-Europe.

f) No snow

left as it'
s become too

warm for this
time of year

g) Warm and wet

ly denying

that white-
amassing Christ

mas mood–time

h) Nothing much

left of that
special day

except the
numerous

i) family-gather

ings the cele

brating dress
ed-up tradit

ional turkey
and the child

j) dren anxious to

discover the

gifts than that
day would trad

itionally fully-
encompass.

Three time *(6)*

a) s Christmas

Oratorio The

Händel Messiah
certainly the

b) strongest most

overpowering

and yet its
arias often

depth a per

c) sonal intimacy

The Bach per
haps the most

unified des
pite its 6

d) separate can

tatas and its

religious ex
pressive

ness as Bach

e) 's works alway

s certifying While

the Schütz the
shortest and

most perfectly

f) sensed with an

unmatched pur

ity signify
ing the Christ

mas blessed
ness.

The darkest (2)

a) time of year

and yet its

brightest Christ
mas message

as if the
one necessi

b) tates the o

ther Man's fall

and the Good
Lord's so im

probable
response.

The pastoral (5)

a) message idealiz

ing the shepherd'

s rural life
untouched by

b) courtly hypo

crisy running

through world
literature

as early as Virgil's

c) Georgios and that

painterly high–
light Poussin'

s Et in Arcadia
Ego But where

d) did it first be

come an inti

mate part of
the musical Christ

mas message perhaps

e) with Corelli

and most all
of the Italian

Baroque or even
pre-Schütz.

Unmention *(4)*

a) able person

al themes re

minding of
that untouch

b) able fruit in

the garden

All-the-more-
tempting It's

man's and wo

c) man's unquench

able curiosity that
has led to high

ly establish
ed civilizat

d) ions but inher

ently to their

decadence
and ulti

mate down-
fall.

Should we (4)

a) present our

selves in our

very-best
for Christ

b) mas when Christ

and his par

ents possessed noth
ing of the

kind poor and
hardly fashion

c) ably dressed

Yes perhaps

to help us
personally

realize how
indifferent

d) The Lord of

all Hosts re

mains to man'
s self-decept

ive appearan
ces.

In the Pass *(4)*

a) over Haggadah

"Why is this
night different
from all o

b) ther night

s" because on

Christmas Eve
The All-Mighty-

God revealed

c) Himself to us

here on earth
in our own

human form
as a helpless

poverty-strick

d) en infant mirr

oring our own
self-import

ant and yet
failing stat

ure.

"The sun (7)

a) also rises"

on this cele

brating Christ
mas Eve morn

b) ing of The

Good Lord's

earthly appear
ance perhaps

to emphasize

c) the true dark

ness of our
own human con

dition and/or
the long dark

d) ly-attuned wait

ing for our

prophetical
ly designat

ed king INRI

e) But dark it

remains in
the midst of

this timely
lifeless call

f) ing a child

of light and

peace is born
to redeem us

from the dark

g) ness of our

so self-import
ant way

s.

Headline (5)

a) s for that

growing bunch

of godless
peoples "Why

b) didn't The

Lord intervene

against all
the evil in

this helpless

c) ly forsaken

world" Perhap
s because he

allowed us the
free will to

realize the

d) fruits of our

own godless
ways the need

to return to
his Shepherd'

e) s fold He

shall return

as He promis
ed at his own

pre–establish
ing time.

My thorough *(3)*

a) ly wrinkled-skin

at 81 as a

tree's ringed
ly enclosing

b) years or per

haps as a

snake ready to
shed it's out

used self-de
ceptive appear

c) ances or per

haps pre-tim

ing me to a
death-warrant

ing future.

It's become (4)

a) increasing

ly difficult

for me to
realize the

b) full scope of

my aging

years At time
s especial

ly with Rose
marie or while

c) writing I feel

myself-re-injuven

ated but when
I all-too-

quickly arise

d) or bend deep

ly-down a hurt
dizziness in

vades the whole
of my now 81

year
s.

Tolerance *(5)*

a) has become al

most a holy

untouchable
word here But

b) it begins as

most all good

qualities
at first at

home Have we

c) learned to

tolerate our
own short-com

ings and have
we found a

d) sufficient

means of re

lieving their
so substan

tial weight
while toleran

e) ce also im

plies a know-

where of one'
s own identi

ty cause.

Breughel (5)

a) the great Christ

ian socially

critical paint
er often make

b) s it difficult

to discover

the whereabout
s of a parti

cular theme

c) as the census

of Caesar August
us Where's Mary

Joseph and the
Christ-child

d) But today here

in Germany

that's all been
previously

solved with the
great exodus of

e) families head

ing home for

Christmas a
most special

family-event.

Family remain (6)

a) ed for my moth

er an almost

sacred–togeth
ernes She even

b) arranged special

cousin's togeth

erness–meeting
s Whereas the

6 Jaffin broth

c) ers newly nam

ed left the
ghetto togeth

er but after
wards never if

d) ever saw each

other again

We 3 children
took to the

Jaffin-side
especially

e) the youngest

spoiled-brat

who even dared
(believe it

or not)
return to

f) the land

of our deadly
persecutor

s to choose
a most love

able wife.

Why are Jew (6)

a) s the most con

tinually suffer

ing of all
peoples also u

b) sually the most

optimistic

as well Is it
like the in

evitable see-
saw when down

c) there's no

way for that

direction
ed so swing

ing back-up
again Or is

d) it perhaps

as with the

prophets
never really

a one-way

e) street at the

other side o
pening-out

vistas of pre-
establishing

f) godly current

ed messianic

expectation
s.

Ode à Eichen *(3)*

a) dorff the great

poet of silen

ce A hushed
stillness

b) pervades his

best poem

s A poet of
the interior

most person
al and inti

c) mate sense

of The Good

Lord's pre-es
tablishing o

therwise
ness.

Great succ (5)

a) esses often

lead one in

to an unlimit
ed feeling

b) of the world'

s–mine–for–

the–asking
unbalancing

that tenta

c) tive crafts

man's re
solve for

a pre–estab
lishing order

ed–sense of

e) now-and-noth

ing-more Such
successes seem

to have eluded
my poetic not-

too-easily-ta

e) ken-path

Should I be
come thankful

for their lack
of an other

wise worldly
acceptance.

"Be happy (3)

    a) fully content

ed with what

you have" Word
s that have re

b) mained with

me from an un

remembered
impersonal

voice Yes I've
been given so

c) much but still

a discontent

ed most de
manding voice

for "more
more more".

Few teen (3)

a) agers includ

ing my once-

self would
have chosen to

b) spend a spec

ial evening

with their
grandparent'

s timely dis
tancing other

c) wise per-inhab

iting no long

er really re
levant world–

sense.

Popular *(4)*

a) music loses

the popular

ity of its
own raison d'

être for the

b) oncoming gener

ation's other
wise need for

self–express
iveness Only

classical music

c) at its most

original–best
continues to

satisfy an
always–present

need for a more

d) limited easily-

dated no long

er tasteful-
response.

And yet a (5)

a) changing time-

oriented taste

can rejudge e
ven re-hear

b) what's no

longer time

ly-relevant
for their

new-born o
therwise-taste

c) Schumann's

denial of

Haydn's great
ness speaks

volumes more
of his own

d) most limited

critical time-

sense than
of Haydn's

actual worth
Now once

e) again on

the newly
reconsider

ed-upswing
ing.

Even if the (3)

a) preacher'

s words are

only a pale
imitation

of The Good

b) Lord's world-

creating word-
invoking pre

sence Still
they can un

bare depthed–

c) levels of

earthy dress
to Christ'

s jewel-shin
ing appear

ance.

The Christian *(4)*

a) faith calendar
ed to Christ's

b) own rhythmic-

appealing

time-urging
s Whereas it'

s also become the

c) churches' own

need for an
ordered time-

sequence imitat
ing perhaps our

d) own personal

ly blood-lev

elled recept
ivity.

It's not (2)

　a) what we feel

however bless

ed that re
sponse may-

have-been
But what He

　b) experienc

ed for our

pre-determin
ing echoing

word-expos
ures.

The right (5)

　a) thing to do

or say isn'

t usually
right-enough

b) for those

really in

need of a
genuine com

forting-em

c) pathy When

our words have
been worn-down

of their orig
inal express

d) iveness as

coins no-long

er-in-use It'
s better than

to respond with

e) touched-hand

s or a silent
I know what

you're exper
iencing.

Why is Christ *(4)*

a) mas usually

celebrated

in most count
ries the-morn

b) ing-after

whereas here

in Germany it'
s the night

of shepherd

c) s and angel

ic praising
s that light

ens the dark
ness of its

d) guilt-amass

ing death-re

sponding
Christ.

Some person *(3)*

a) s simply

must take

to the oppos
ite end of an

arguable pur

b) posing It

may be in
their nature

and/or be
cause of a
genuine uncer

c) tainty or e

ven because
we've treaded

on ground
holy-for-them.

Is Christ *(3)*

a) mas an end

or a beginn

ing The end
of Israel'

s still long-

b) awaited Mess

iah and the
beginning of

a new self-
fulfilling

era Christ

c) the A and O

end and be
ginning of

time's and
of our very-

being.

In Nomine
Domini!

Christmas
Day 2018

Poetry books by David Jaffin

1. **Conformed to Stone,** Abelard-Schuman, New York 1968, London 1970.

2. **Emptied Spaces,** with an illustration by Jacques Lipschitz, Abelard-Schuman, London 1972.

3. **In the Glass of Winter,** Abelard-Schuman, London 1975, with an illustration by Mordechai Ardon.

4. **As One,** The Elizabeth Press, New Rochelle, N. Y. 1975.

5. **The Half of a Circle,** The Elizabeth Press, New Rochelle, N. Y. 1977.

6. **Space of,** The Elizabeth Press, New Rochelle, N. Y. 1978.

7. **Preceptions,** The Elizabeth Press, New Rochelle, N. Y. 1979.

8. **For the Finger's Want of Sound,** Shearsman Plymouth, England 1982.

9. **The Density for Color,** Shearsman Plymouth, England 1982.

10. **Selected Poems** with an illustration by Mordechai Ardon, English/Hebrew, Massada Publishers, Givatyim, Israel 1982.

11. **The Telling of Time,** Shearsman Books, Kentisbeare, England 2000 and Johannis, Lahr, Germany.

12. **That Sense for Meaning,** Shearsman Books, Kentisbeare, England 2001 and Johannis, Lahr, Germany.

13. **Into the timeless Deep,** Shearsman Books, Kentisbeare, England 2003 and Johannis, Lahr, Germany.

14. **A Birth in Seeing,** Shearsman Books, Exeter, England 2003 and Johannis, Lahr, Germany.

15. **Through Lost Silences,** Shearsman Books, Exeter, England 2003 and Johannis, Lahr, Germany.

16. **A voiced Awakening,** Shearsman Books, Exter, England 2004 and Johannis, Lahr, Germany.

17. **These Time-Shifting Thoughts**, Shearsman Books, Exeter, England 2005 and Johannis, Lahr, Germany.

18. **Intimacies of Sound,** Shearsman Books, Exeter, England 2005 and Johannis, Lahr, Germany.

19. **Dream Flow** with an illustration by Charles Seliger, Shearsman Books, Exeter, England 2006 and Johannis, Lahr, Germany.

20. **Sunstreams** with an illustration by Charles Seliger, Shearsman Books, Exeter, England 2007 and Johannis, Lahr, Germany.

21. **Thought Colors,** with an illustration by Charles Seliger, Shearsman Books, Exeter, England 2008 and Johannis, Lahr, Germany.

22. **Eye-Sensing,** Ahadada, Tokyo, Japan and Toronto, Canada 2008.

23. **Wind-phrasings,** with an illustration by Charles Seliger, Shearsman Books, Exeter, England 2009 and Johannis, Lahr, Germany.

24. **Time shadows,** with an illustration by Charles Seliger, Shearsman Books, Exeter, England 2009 and Johannis, Lahr, Germany.

25. **A World mapped-out,** with an illustration by Charles Seliger, Shearsman Books, Exeter, England 2010.

26. **Light Paths,** with an illustration by Charles Seliger, Shearsman Books, Exeter, England 2011 and Edition Wortschatz, Schwarzenfeld, Germany.

27. **Always Now,** with an illustration by Charles Seliger, Shearsman Books, Bristol, England 2012 and Edition Wortschatz, Schwarzenfeld, Germany.

28. **Labyrinthed,** with an illustration by Charles Seliger, Shearsman Books, Bristol, England 2012 and Edition Wortschatz, Schwarzenfeld, Germany.

29. **The Other Side of Self,** with an illustration by Charles Seliger, Shearsman Books, Bristol, England 2012 and Edition Wortschatz, Schwarzenfeld, Germany.

30. **Light Sources,** with an illustration by Charles Seliger, Shearsman Books, Bristol, England 2013 and Edition Wortschatz, Schwarzenfeld, Germany.

31. **Landing Rights,** with an illustration by Charles Seliger, Shearsman Books, Bristol, England 2014 and Edition Wortschatz, Schwarzenfeld, Germany.

32. **Listening to Silence,** with an illustration by Charles Seliger, Shearsman Books, Bristol, England 2014 and Edition Wortschatz, Schwarzenfeld, Germany.

33. **Taking Leave,** with an illustration by Mei Fêng, Shearsman Books, Bristol, England 2014 and Edition Wortschatz, Schwarzenfeld, Germany.

34. **Jewel Sensed,** with an illustration by Paul Klee, Shearsman Books, Bristol, England 2015 and Edition Wortschatz, Schwarzenfeld, Germany.

35. **Shadowing Images**, with an illustration by Pieter de Hooch, Shearsman Books, Bristol, England 2015 and Edition Wortschatz, Schwarzenfeld.

36. **Untouched Silences**, with an illustration by Paul Seehaus, Shearsman Books, Bristol, England 2016 and Edition Wortschatz, Schwarzenfeld.

37. **Soundlesss Impressions**, with an illustration by Qi Baishi, Shearsman Books, Bristol, England 2016 and Edition Wortschatz, Schwarzenfeld.

38. **Moon Flowers**, with a photograph by Hannelore Bäumler, Shearsman Books, Bristol, England 2017 and Edition Wortschatz, Schwarzenfeld.

39. **The Healing of a Broken World**, with a photograph by Hannelore Bäumler, Shearsman Books, Bristol, England 2018 and Edition Wortschatz, Cuxhaven.

40. **Opus 40**, with a photograph by Hannelore Bäumler, Shearsman Books, Bristol, England 2018 and Edition Wortschatz, Cuxhaven.

41. **Identity Cause**, with a photograph by Hannelore Bäumler, Shearsman Books, Bristol, England 2018 and Edition Wortschatz, Cuxhaven.

42. **Kaleidoscope**, with a photograph by Hannelore Bäumler, Shearsman Books, Bristol, England 2019 and Edition Wortschatz, Cuxhaven.

Book on David Jaffin's poetry: Warren Fulton, **Poemed on a beach,** Ahadada, Tokyo, Japan and Toronto, Canada 2010.